CONTENTS

Natural
FAMILY
PLANNING

A Catholic Approach

Mary Lee Barron PhD, RN, FNP-BC

Liguori
ONE LIGUORI DRIVE
LIGUORI MO 63057-9999

Imprimi Potest:
Thomas D. Picton, C.Ss.R.
Provincial, Denver Province
The Redemptorists

Imprimatur:
Most Reverend Robert J. Hermann
Archdiocesan Administrator, Archdiocese of St. Louis

ISBN 978-0-7648-1833-2
© 2009, Liguori Publications

Printed in the United States of America
13 12 11 10 09   5 4 3 2 1

Anatomical illustration on page 21 is from *Marquette Manual of NFP* by Richard Fehring, PhD, RN. Copyright © 1999, Marquette Institute of Natural Family Planning. All rights reserved. Used by permission of Marquette Institute of Natural Family Planning, Milwaukee, WI.

Scripture texts in this work are taken from the *New American Bible with Revised New Testament and Revised Psalms* © 1991, 1986, 1970 Confraternity of Christian Doctrine, Washington, D.C. and are used by permission of the copyright owner. All Rights Reserved. No part of the *New American Bible* may be reproduced in any form without permission in writing from the copyright owner.

Excerpts from *Vatican Council II: The Basic Sixteen Documents,* Revised Translation, copyright 1996 by Reverend Austin Flannery, OP; and *Vatican II: More Post Conciliar Documents,* New Revised Edition, copyright 1982, 1998 by Reverend Austin Flannery, OP; published by Costello Publishing Company, Inc., Northport, NY, are used by permission of the publisher, all rights reserved.

Excerpts from English translation of the *Catechism of the Catholic Church* for the United States of America © 1994, United States Catholic Conference, Inc.—Libreria Editrice Vaticana; English translation of the *Catechism of the Catholic Church: Modifications from the Editio Typica* © 1997, United States Catholic Conference, Inc.—Libreria Editrice Vaticana.

Liguori Publications, a nonprofit corporation, is an apostolate of the Redemptorists. To learn more about the Redemptorists, visit Redemptorists.com.

To order, call 800-325-9521.
www.liguori.org

INTRODUCTION

I write this booklet from the perspectives of a Catholic lay-woman, wife, mother, nurse practitioner specializing in women's health, and natural family planning (NFP) educator.

As an NFP teacher, I encounter couples preparing for marriage as well as couples who are already married. Some already use contraceptives, not realizing how contraceptive use affects their relationship and their faith and how chemical contraceptives affect the woman's body. It's ironic that, even in this age of information and arguments about "comprehensive sexual education," couples seem to know little about how their bodies work or how contraceptives work. Health care professionals have an obligation to advise patients of possible side effects and the action of all medications, but it's also each person's responsibility to be informed about the medications he or she takes.

Some couples I encounter have already decided to use NFP, and I've been blessed to hear their testimonies about the positive effects of NFP on their marriages. They're frequently joyful and generous with each other and with others. And they've discovered an unexpected bonus to NFP: Women who chart their cycles know how their bodies work, and health care professionals find the detailed information in their charts of great value as they care for them.

All of the couples in my classes come to realize that if they want to fully live out their marriage covenant and practice chastity within their marriage, the Church is ready to help them realize that goal.

The other reasons for using NFP go beyond biology, and I'll explain the faith perspective of NFP. If you allow those reasons to touch your heart, you'll be open to understanding the marriage covenant as rooted in the beauty of God's commands:

> *What we do with our bodies expresses our deepest held convictions about ourselves, God, the meaning of love, and the ordering of the universe. When the Church's sacramental view of the body is taken seriously, we understand that sexual union is not only a biological process, but a profound theological process: "This is a great mystery, but I speak in reference to Christ and the church"* (Ephesians 5:32).[1]

This booklet is only an introduction to NFP, and after reading it you'll no doubt have questions. Please seek more information from a health care professional, NFP educator, and/or clergy.

Notes

1. West, Christopher. 2003. "God, Sex, and Babies: What the Church *Really* Teaches about Responsible Parenthood." *This Rock* 14, no. 9 (November), www.catholic.com/ thisrock/2003/0311fea3.asp (accessed April 3, 2009).

CATHOLIC TEACHING

Marital Love

> *God created man in his image; in the divine image he created him; male and female he created them. God blessed them, saying: "Be fertile and multiply"* (Genesis 1: 27–28).

The creation story is a call to love. When we read the story of Adam and Eve before the fall, we understand God's original call to us—a call not only of love, but also of beauty, a call in which we give ourselves completely to one another. And notice that God's *first* command to humankind was to "be fertile and multiply."

After the fall, Adam and Eve realized they were naked and tried to cover themselves. The original relationship was altered. That vision of the beauty of what God created us to be is now what we strive for in our relationships. We feel this in our deepest longings: to love and be loved. In this passage from Genesis, man and woman are created for unity. They become one flesh. This love is first of all fully human; that is, it involves both the body and the spirit. The man and woman join their hearts and souls as well as their bodies (Paul VI, Encyclical Letter on the Regulation of Births[1]; *Humanae Vitae [HV]*, 9) in the image of God. This special relationship is a choice both the man and the woman must be free to make.

Marriage between baptized persons represents the union of Christ and the Church (*HV* 8). Marital love is to be total, faithful, exclusive, and indissoluble. During the Catholic Rite of Marriage, the couple is asked whether they are there of their own accord, whether they will be faithful until they die, and whether they intend to accept the children God gives them. That is, marriage is total self-giving *only* to one another and *for life.*

As Jesus stated, "So they are no longer two, but one flesh. Therefore, what God has joined together, no human being must separate" (Matthew 19:6.) Because we are images of God, and because God has created this relationship by his divine love, the Church looks on the relationship of a married couple as a vocation that is noble, sacred, and sacramental.

The sacrament of marriage is the original means of holiness for Christian married couples and families (John Paul II, The Christian Family in the Modern World; *Familiaris Consortio (FC)*, 56).[2] The marriage bond isn't to be viewed as a burden or something imposed by God upon us. The grace of the sacrament helps the couple live with each other, to follow Christ, to know joy, to endure sorrow and hardships, to forgive each other, and to nurture one another and their mutual love. The joy of their love and family life is a preview of heaven (*Catechism of the Catholic Church*, 1641–1642).[3]

The Meaning of the Body

Pope John Paul II said the human body is representative of God and all his mysteries. God uses our bodies to reveal the truth of himself. Jesus teaches us that the meaning of life is in loving one another: "Love one another as I love you" (John 15:12).

How did Christ love us? He gave up his life for us. God's love for us is made flesh in Jesus Christ. Christ's love is a reality of the body. Thus, in the gift of our bodies to one another, we act on our love as Christ loved us. The body alone is capable of making visible what is invisible: the spiritual and divine. The body reveals God's invisible mystery.

Married love, then, is different from any other love. By the very nature of the two becoming one, this kind of love is ordered toward God and one another; creating new life together is cooperating with God's design. Marital love is unitive and procreative, that is, love-giving and life-giving. Sexual acts between husband and wife are representations of God's love for his creation. God's love for us is never sterile. Thus, the expression of love that takes place between married people must never be intentionally sterile.

Children Are Gifts From God

> *Children too are a gift from the LORD, the fruit of the womb, a reward. Like arrows in the hand of a warrior are the children born in one's youth. Blessed are they whose quivers are full. They will never be shamed contending with foes at the gate* (Psalm 127:3-5).

In general, those who argue for contraception start with the result, the fruit of marital union, a view in which children are seen as a negative. In our culture's ideal image, most families are pictured with two children, preferably one boy and one girl. Unplanned pregnancy occurs in 50 percent of couples who use contraceptives, and the solution always includes more contraceptives. Abortion is offered as the solution when contraception fails (Casey v Planned Parenthood, 1992).

The problem with approaching this issue from the direction of the result is that it leaves out discussion of causes and the decision-making or behaviors that led to the fruit.

The Church approaches the matter from the opposite direction, starting with the holiness of the marital act itself—what it means and what it was intended for. These two meanings, life-giving and love-giving, cannot willfully be separated any more than Christ's sacrifice can be separated from our redemption.

Our culture of death calls pregnancy and children "contraceptive failures." Generating new life and the beauty of God's creation should never be thought of as a "failure."

Intentions

Some would say that using contraceptives is no different than abstaining from intercourse during the fertile time because the ends are the same. However, the ends never justify the means. Couples using contraceptives willfully suppress their fertility. They are saying with their bodies, "I love you, but I don't love all of you. I don't love your fertility." Couples who use NFP aren't practicing contraception—by giving themselves completely to one another in body and soul, they're preserving the integrity of the sacrament.

In God's design, women are naturally infertile for many days of the menstrual cycle. The marital act during these times promotes bonding and yet is open to new life. There is no sin in abstaining from the marital act. In fact, on occasion couples choose to do just that…during times of sickness or stress, for example.

And what of those couples who have a serious reason to avoid pregnancy? Are couples supposed to leave their family size to chance? The Church has no expectation that couples do so. In addressing the issue of responsible parenthood (*HV* 10), the Church has said couples may choose to have a large family or not. That's up to the couple alone. The Church encourages couples to make that decision in the spirit of generosity, but with responsibility to God, to each other, to the children already born, and to society.

Reasons to limit family size may include physical, economic, psychological, and social conditions with respect to moral law. God gave us the intelligence to regulate our fertility, but that decision must be made in a moral way.

Formation of Conscience

To avoid evil, we must make the effort to find out what is true and good; therefore, the Church calls on everyone to appropriately form his or her conscience. Conscience formation is a lifelong process. "A well-formed conscience is upright and truthful" (*CCC* 1783). It helps us make right judgments in accord with reason and God's laws.

The Church is there to help us with our moral decision-making and to explain why some decisions are well-grounded and spiritually good and why others are not. Think of all the resources at our disposal: priestly advice and homilies, the sacraments, Catholic education, the *Catechism of the Catholic Church*, Church documents, and the gifts of the Holy Spirit.

NFP As a Gift

NFP is a means for learning to live with fertility. Fertility isn't a disease.

Many couples find that living an NFP lifestyle gives them a better understanding of their fertility, frees them from fear of medical side effects, increases their communication, encourages a greater sense of sharing and a generosity to life, fosters their sexual self-control, and gives them the peace of following their spiritual, religious, cultural, and/or ethical beliefs.

NFP requires couples to deeply revere each other, respect each other's bodies, and develop additional ways of communicating their love. Periodic abstinence encourages couples to focus on aspects of their relationship beyond the physical and results in a "honeymoon effect." Holistic sexuality isn't just physical—it has spiritual, emotional, and psychological facets. Neither spouse takes the other for granted.

The mutual cooperation and motivation NFP fosters often carry over to other areas. Couples find that when they can communicate about their intentions with NFP, it's easier to discuss other issues such as finances, child-rearing, and family.

The most important benefit of NFP is that it allows spouses to live the mutual gift of self that is an essential element of marriage. The Church values marital sexual love. NFP allows us to be authentic in the expression of that love.

Notes

1. Paul VI. 1968. Encyclical Letter on the Regulation of Birth *(Humanae Vitae)*. www.vatican.va/offices/index.htm (accessed April 3, 2009).
2. John Paul II. 1981. The Christian Family in the Modern World *(Familiaris Consortio)*. www.vatican.va/offices/index.htm (accessed April 3, 2009).
3. *Catechism of the Catholic Church*. 1994. Washington, DC: United States Catholic Conference, Inc. www.usccb.org/catechism/text/ (accessed April 3, 2009).

BACKGROUND

Twentieth-Century Theological Developments

Many Christians don't realize that before 1930, *all* Christian churches opposed contraception as unnatural and therefore an interference with God's design for human sexuality. This common and constant teaching changed in 1930 at the Lambeth Conference, when Anglicans permitted the use of contraceptives on a limited basis—for grave reasons only. Other denominations rapidly absorbed this change. In response, Pope Pius XI published his encyclical On Christian Marriage *(Casti Connubii)*[1] on December 31, 1930.

This encyclical is a beautiful explanation of Christian teaching on marriage and birth control and on preserving the purity and chastity of the marital union. Pius XI said that in interfering with the natural outcome of marital relations—conceiving a baby— use of contraception was an offense against the laws of God and nature. He clearly reaffirmed the teaching that contraception was a grave sin *(CC* 56).

Questions about the morality of confining marital sexual relations to the infertile time had been addressed to the Vatican during the last half of the 1800s, and the practice had been approved even before its scientific basis had been discovered. Pius XI viewed abstaining during the fertile time as morally acceptable (*CC* 59).

Since then, the doctrine has had further support from Paul VI (*Humanae Vitae*), John Paul II (*Familiaris Consortio, Veritatis Splendor*), the Congregation for the Doctrine of the Faith (The Dignity of a Person [*Dignitas Personae*]), and many others.

With the appearance of the first oral contraceptives in 1960, some in the Church argued for reconsideration of Catholic teaching. In 1963 Pope John XXIII established a Papal Birth Control Commission of six European nontheologians. Pope Paul VI added theologians to the commission and over the next three years expanded it to seventy-two members from five continents, including three married couples.

In 1965 the Second Vatican Council published Pastoral Constitution on the Church in the Modern World (*Gaudium et Spes*).[2] This document discusses the true meaning of our humanity and the dignity of the human person as created in the image of God. The sexual nature of men and women surpasses that of lower forms of life. Marital intimacy should be respected and ordered to human dignity. The Council Fathers recognized that at times couples might need to limit or space children but that this must be done with openness to life and with marital chastity, not with artificial methods of birth control (51).

Before Paul VI published his 1968 Encyclical Letter on the Regulation of Birth (*Humanae Vitae*),[3] many had expected him to overturn the long-held teaching of the Church. However, *Humanae Vitae* specifically states that periodic continence (refraining from intercourse), far from harming conjugal love, confers on it a higher human value by fostering attention to one's partner, driving out selfishness, creating a deepening sense of responsibility, providing a more effective education for children, and enriching marriage with spiritual values, serenity, and peace (21).

Paul VI prophetically wrote that acceptance of artificial birth control methods would result in several negative consequences, among them a "general lowering of moral standards" resulting from sex without consequences, the danger that men could reduce women "to being a mere instrument for the satisfaction of [their] own desires," and an abuse of power by public authorities in undermining families (*HV* 17).

Paul VI was criticized for linking sterilization and abortion to contraception, yet abortion was legalized in the United States less than five years later. And China's one-child policy proves that artificial birth control can be used by governments to impose population control.

John Paul II continued the papal stand against contraception with a series of lectures on the theology of the body[4] in which he talked about the original unity between man and woman, purity of heart, marriage, and celibacy, focusing mainly on responsible parenthood and marital chastity. He specifically described the practice of artificial contraception as an act not permitted by Catholic teaching in any circumstances. His encyclical *Veritatis Splendor*[5] also clarifies the use of conscience in arriving at moral decisions, including the use of contraception.

In 1987 the Congregation for the Doctrine of the Faith released the Instruction on Respect for Human Life in Its Origin and on the Dignity of Procreation: Replies to Certain Questions of the Day (*Donum Vitae*).[6] This document affirmed that from the moment of conception, the life of every human being is to be respected in an absolute way and the spiritual soul of each human being is created by God. Human life bears the image of God and is sacred (18), and it will always have a special relationship with God (19). No human being has the right to destroy another (20).

Because of the dignity of both the child and of the parents, *Donum Vitae* declares that *in vitro* fertilization is always wrong.

While desiring a child of their own is good and natural, a couple does not have the right to one by any means. A child is a gift, not a thing that adults have a right to manufacture, manipulate, or destroy. A child is a person whose individual rights and dignity must be respected and safeguarded. A child has the right to be born and raised within marriage (*DV* 35).

In 1995, John Paul II's encyclical On the Value and Inviolability of Human Life (*Evangelium Vitae*)[7] introduced the terms "culture of life" and "culture of death" (21). Beginning with an overview of past and present threats to human life, the encyclical gives a brief history of the many biblical prohibitions against killing, then addresses abortion, euthanasia, and the death penalty in light of these biblical passages. The encyclical emphasizes the importance of a society built around the family rather than a wish to improve efficiency and stresses our duty to care for the poor and the sick. We are called to transform our culture by forming our consciences to value the worth of every human life. We must re-establish the connection between life and freedom, which are inseparable. When life isn't valued, freedom cannot exist; and life can't be lived to the fullest without freedom (125).

In 2008 the Congregation for the Doctrine of the Faith maintained the dignity of all human life, marriage, and human reproduction with the instruction, The Dignity of a Person (*Dignitas Personae*),[8] in which the two key principles of *Donum Vitae* and *Evangelium Vitae* are reaffirmed and applied to new questions generated by further scientific technology:

- The human being is to be respected and treated as a person with rights from the moment of conception. (4).
- Procreation of children must take place in marriage (6).
- Techniques to assist couples are morally permissible if they respect life, the physical integrity of men and women,

and the unity of marriage. Procreation must result from the marital act specific to the love of a husband and wife. Medical therapy should focus on treating the cause of infertility rather than on using technology to take the place of the marital act in conceiving a child (12–13).

Scientific Developments

The timing of ovulation in the menstrual cycle was discovered in the 1920s independently by two researchers: Dr. Herman Knaus of Germany and Dr. Kyusaku Ogino of Japan.

Dr. Knaus designed the first calendar method of birth control based on the idea that ovulation precedes menstruation by about two weeks. An American physician, Dr. Leo Latz of Loyola University in Chicago, studied with Dr. Knaus and subsequently published the first manual, *The Rhythm of Sterility and Fertility in Women*, in 1932. Dr. Latz wanted couples to be able to learn this method within three minutes. His research, published in 1942,[9] reported 15,924 cycles with no pregnancies. The calendar "rhythm" method of the 1930s to the 1950s was considered a fairly effective form of family planning.

In the 1930s, Wilhelm Hillebrand, a German Catholic priest, developed a system for avoiding pregnancy based on basal body temperature. Both of these methods were widely used into the 1960s by Catholic couples.

Over time, as more knowledge of menstrual-cycle events developed, additional elements were used to judge the timing of ovulation. These included cervical-mucus observation, urinary hormone measurement, and chemical changes in the woman's body. Essentially, NFP moved from calculations of the fertile time based on the length of the cycle to calculations based on many markers.

The modern era of NFP really began with the development of the Billings Ovulation Method in the 1960s. This method was introduced in the United States in 1970.

Unfortunately, modern NFP is often dismissed as the rhythm method, which was largely abandoned in the 1960s. With more scientific knowledge of the menstrual cycle and variations among women, modern-day NFP is highly effective for avoiding *or* achieving pregnancy.

In support of Church teaching, lay organizations such as the Couple to Couple League and professional organizations were formed to promote public awareness of NFP. Because no corporations will make money from NFP, there are no sales representatives to pass out information on NFP as there are for artificial contraceptives. Physicians and nurses may have minimal and/or inaccurate schooling on the technique and benefits because it's easier to prescribe artificial contraceptives than to teach NFP. Even Catholic colleges inconsistently include NFP in their curriculum, and clergy rarely preach on the topic. However, when those who use NFP are surveyed, the response is overwhelmingly positive.[10]

Many dioceses actively promote NFP in marriage-preparation programs and offices of NFP and by allotting funds for teaching couples and educating NFP teachers. The United States Conference of Catholic Bishops has an office devoted to NFP issues (see page 45) and publishes a forum for current NFP medical research.

Notes

1. Pius XI. 1930. On Christian Marriage *(Casti Connubii)*. www. vatican.va/offices/index.htm (accessed April 3, 2009).
2. Paul VI. 1965. Pastoral Constitution on the Church in the Modern World *(Gaudium et Spes)*. www.vatican.va/offices/ index.htm (accessed April 3, 2009).
3. Paul VI. 1968. Encyclical Letter on the Regulation of Birth *(Humanae Vitae)*. www.vatican.va/offices/index.htm (accessed April 3, 2009).
4. John Paul II. 2006. *Man and Woman He Created Them: A Theology of the Body.* Boston: Pauline Books and Media.
5. John Paul II. 1993. *Veritatis Splendor.* www.vatican.va/offices/ index.htm (accessed April 3, 2009).
6. Congregation for the Doctrine of the Faith. 1987. Instruction on Respect for Human Life in Its Origin and on the Dignity of Procreation: Replies to Certain Questions of the Day (*Donum Vitae*). www.vatican.va/offices/index.htm (accessed April 3, 2009).
7. John Paul II. 1995. On the Value and Inviolability of Human Life (*Evangelium Vitae*). www.vatican.va/offices/index.htm (accessed April 3, 2009).
8. Congregation for the Doctrine of the Faith, Instruction *Dignitas Personae* on Certain Bioethical Questions (Sept. 8, 2008).
9. Latz LJ and Reiner E. 1942. Further studies on the sterile and fertile periods in women. *American Journal of Obstetrics and Gynecology,* 43:74–79.
10. VandeVusse L, Hanson L, Fehring RJ, et al. 2003. Couples' Views of the Effects of Natural Family Planning on Marital Dynamics. *Journal of Nursing Scholarship,* 35:2, 171–176.

NFP METHODS

The United States Conference of Catholic Bishops defines NFP as follows:

> *Methods for achieving and avoiding pregnancies...based on the observation of the naturally occurring signs and symptoms of the fertile and infertile phases of the menstrual cycle.*
>
> *Couples using natural family planning methods to avoid pregnancy abstain from intercourse and genital contact during the fertile phase of the woman's cycle. No drugs, devices, or surgical procedures are used to avoid pregnancy.*
>
> *NFP reflects the dignity of the human person within the context of marriage and family life, and promotes openness to life and the gift of the child. By complementing the love-giving and life-giving nature of marriage, NFP can enrich the bond between husband and wife.*[1]

If the couple is trying to avoid pregnancy, they must abstain from intercourse during the fertile window. For this reason, NFP is sometimes referred to as *periodic abstinence*. Other terms include *fertility awareness* and *fertility appreciation*.

But NFP is more than just monitoring biologic markers—it's learning to live with fertility. When a husband and wife use

NFP appropriately, they *share* responsibility for living with their combined fertility. NFP is a healthy and holistic way to plan for children.

An added benefit is that women who chart their menstrual cycles find it easier to monitor their health and detect problems.

Female Anatomy

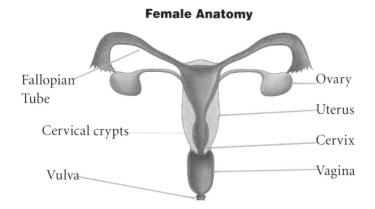

Fallopian Tube

Cervical crypts

Vulva

Ovary

Uterus

Cervix

Vagina

Signs of Fertility

A normal menstrual cycle ranges from twenty-one to thirty-five days and has three phases: *preovulatory infertility, fertile window,* and *postovulatory infertility.* All NFP methods identify these phases so the information can be used to avoid or achieve pregnancy.

The typical man is always fertile. Sperm can survive in a woman's body for up to five days, so she is considered fertile before she ovulates. Ovulation typically occurs nine to seventeen days before a menstrual period is due to occur, and the egg can live for 12 to 24 hours after ovulation.

Several days before ovulation, the hormone *estrogen* causes the woman's cervix to produce a stretchy, clear (like egg white) mucus that supports the life of the sperm by channeling it toward the uterus. Sperm can live three to five days in good-quality cervical mucus.

A surge of luteinizing hormone causes the ovary to release an egg (*ovulation*) as well as the hormone *progesterone*, which raises the woman's body temperature by about a half degree Fahrenheit and causes thickening of the cervical mucus.

Unless it's fertilized, the egg dies within twelve to twenty-four hours after ovulation. Therefore, the fertile window is approximately six days.

Some women have irregular menstrual cycles, meaning the cycles vary in length by more than two weeks: one cycle might be twenty-one days and the next occurs more than thirty-five days later. Cycles more than forty-two days apart are often irregular. A cycle that varies by a few days is very common and quite normal.

Any woman can use NFP no matter how irregular her cycles. She can track her fertility signs during breastfeeding as well as at other times when cycles are typically irregular (during perimenopause, for example).

Single-Index NFP Methods

In the *ovulation, two-day,* and *calendar-based* methods, fertility is tracked by observing only one marker.

OVULATION METHOD

Several versions of this method, which involves daily monitoring and tracking of cervical-mucus characteristics, are taught in the United States: the *Billings Ovulation Method, Creighton Model FertilityCare System,* and *Family of the Americas Foundation Method.*

Billings Ovulation Method (BOM)

Introduced in the 1960s, this method relies on the woman's perception of vulvar sensation and self-examination for the detection of the change in cervical-mucus characteristics during the menstrual cycle.

After the menstrual period, a variable number of "dry" days when no mucus can be detected is followed by increasingly detectable sensation changes and an increase in mucus. A few days later, the volume of mucus significantly increases, becoming more watery and slippery. The amount of slippery mucus peaks just before or at ovulation. These changes are entered daily on a specially designed chart.

The method is taught in a two-class series with follow-up appointments every two to three weeks while the couples become confident in their charting and use of the method. Women are able to learn the method quite rapidly: In a large five-country study supported by the World Health Organization,[2] 94 percent of women were able to detect changes in their cervical mucus after three teaching cycles; 91 percent were rated as having good or excellent understanding of the method after just one teaching cycle.

Originally called the Ovulation Method, the name "Billings" was added to the title by the World Health Organization to identify the method as using the original format and materials developed by Australian doctors John and Lyn Billings.

BOM is taught all over the world. Teachers must attend training workshops and do a supervised practicum of at least six months. They needn't be health care professionals. The teacher-training course meets Diocesan Development Standards and is approved by the United States Conference of Catholic Bishops.

Creighton Model FertilityCare System (CrM)

Introduced in 1976 by Dr. Thomas Hilgers, CrM teaches women to observe cervical mucus to monitor their reproductive health and identify times of fertility and infertility. Although described by Dr. Hilgers as a standardization of BOM, the cervical-mucus observation technique, type, and charting are different. The method is taught in nine sessions—one introductory and eight follow-up—spread over the first year of use.

CrM teachers, known as FertilityCare practitioners, attend a 13-month training program. FertilityCare practitioners needn't be health care professionals, although many are. CrM is taught primarily in English-speaking countries—United States, Ireland, and Australia—but a Spanish version is available. The teacher-training course meets Diocesan Development Standards and is approved by the United States Conference of Catholic Bishops.

Family of the Americas Foundation Method (FAF)

This simplified method is based on BOM. The charting involves pictures and natural colors, for example, brown for infertile rather than the green color used by BOM. Wetness (fertility) is represented by a picture stamp of rain drops.

The FAF method is taught around the world and has been translated into twenty-one languages. Teachers needn't be health care professionals. Teachers attend a training course and do a minimum six-month supervised practicum. The teacher-training course meets Diocesan Development Standards and is approved by the United States Conference of Catholic Bishops.

TWO-DAY METHOD OF FERTILITY AWARENESS

In this method, cervical secretions are monitored every day. If mucus is present on the current *or* previous day, the woman considers herself fertile. If mucus is not present on the current *and* previous day, she considers herself infertile. This method is quite easy to use and teach. One session is required to learn the method from an NFP teacher. At times—during breastfeeding, for example—the method has limitations.

CALENDAR-BASED METHOD
Standard Days Method (SDM)

A variation on the calendar-rhythm method, SDM is strictly meant for women with regular menstrual cycles of twenty-six to thirty-two days **only**. The woman moves a ring over a series of color-coded beads (CycleBeads) that represent the fertile and infertile days, having or avoiding intercourse on fertile days (eight through nineteen) depending on whether the couple is trying to achieve or avoid pregnancy.

The method is quickly learned and doesn't require the woman to be literate. The method was designed and researched by George-town University's Institute of Reproductive Health and tested in several third-world countries.

Multi-Index Methods

In the *sympto-thermal* and *hormonal-monitoring* methods, fertility is tracked by observing more than one marker.

SYMPTO-THERMAL METHOD

The primary fertility signs observed in this method are *basal body temperature* (BBT), *cervical mucus*, and *calendar calculations*. Secondary signs include a change in cervical position, breast tenderness or sensitivity, lymph node swelling in the groin, abdominal pain, and/or swelling of the vulva. When the primary fertility signs are recorded on a chart, these secondary signs are noted and used to determine that ovulation is taking place.

A woman practicing symptoms-based fertility awareness can choose to observe one or several signs. The most common approach is to combine cervical-mucus observation and BBT patterns.

STM emphasizes the relationship between BBT and the presence of cervical mucus. BBT readings are taken immediately on awakening at approximately the same time every morning. BBT remains low before ovulation, at which it generally increases by 0.5 to 1.0 degree Fahrenheit. When the BBT remains elevated for three consecutive days, the fertile phase of the cycle has passed. Monitoring more than one biological sign serves as a double-check for the beginning, peak, and end of the fertile phase.

Due to problems with mercury in traditional thermometers, BBT readings are best done with a digital thermometer. Sophisticated electronic thermometers like the Baby-Comp and Lady-Comp electronically record BBT and calendar rhythm to identify the infertile and fertile days of the menstrual cycle.

STM is taught in several formats in the United States. Two examples are the Couple to Couple League and Northwest Family Services. Couples attend two to three training sessions with follow-up until they can confidently chart their fertility signs. Teaching couples needn't be health care professionals. In general, teaching couples attend a workshop, spend a specified number of hours in self-study, pass an examination, and do a minimum six-month supervised practicum teaching a specified number of couples.

HORMONAL-MONITORING METHOD

Electronic fertility monitors were introduced in the 1990s. The monitor currently available in the United States is the Clearblue Easy Fertility Monitor, a handheld electronic device that uses disposable test strips. A woman dips the wick end of a test stick in her first morning urine sample. She places the stick in the monitor, which "reads" the levels of urinary estrogen and luteinizing hormone (the hormone that causes the ovary to release an egg).

The monitor indicates three levels of fertility: low, high, and peak. The fertile phase begins when the estrogen level rises (high fertility). The fertile phase ends three days after the highest level of luteinizing hormone (peak fertility).

In the United States, the Clearblue Easy Fertility Monitor is approved for use in achieving pregnancy. However, by using it "backward," many couples have avoided pregnancy. Certain features make its use for avoiding pregnancy best taught by an NFP teacher.[3]

Marquette Method

Developed in 1999, this method incorporates the use of all primary fertility signs. Couples are instructed in the use of cervical-mucus observation, BBT measurement, and the Clearblue Easy Fertility Monitor. Couples choose which sign they wish to use, with many choosing a combination of cervical mucus and the fertility monitor. Others choose to use all signs, and some use the monitor only. Charts that accommodate the couple's sign preference are provided in the class materials. Adaptations for use of the monitor during breastfeeding and with long menstrual cycles have been developed.

The Marquette Method is taught in two to three classroom sessions with private follow-up until the couple feels confident. Many couples learn the method rapidly. The Marquette Method must be taught by a nurse or physician trained in a graduate-level or continuing-education course at Marquette University College of Nursing or a continuing education course at Saint Louis University.

Classes are followed by an examination and a minimum six-month practicum. The teacher-training course meets Diocesan Development Standards and is approved by the United States Conference of Catholic Bishops.

NFP During Breastfeeding

The assistance of an NFP teacher during breastfeeding is important because menstrual periods may be absent and fertility signs a little more difficult to interpret. The return of fertility is associated with

- less-frequent breastfeeding;
- addition of foods to baby's diet;
- decreased sucking time;
- baby sleeps through the night; and
- anxiety, stress, or illness.

LACTATIONAL AMENORRHEA METHOD (LAM)

This method of avoiding pregnancy is based on the natural post-partum infertility that occurs when a woman is fully breastfeeding and not yet having periods. Under the following circumstances, LAM is 98 percent to 99.5 percent effective during the first six months after giving birth[4]:

- Breastfeeding is the infant's only (or almost only) source of nutrition.
- The infant breast feeds at least every four hours during the day and at least every six hours at night.
- The infant is less than six months old.
- Menstrual periods have not returned.

Choosing a Method

While NFP can be learned from a book, couples will benefit more from taking a class (online or in person) that offers follow-up with an NFP teacher. Effectiveness of NFP is related to the expertise of the couple and teacher as well as understanding of the method.

The choice of an NFP method is partially dependent on what is available in the area. The United States Conference of Catholic Bishops has an extensive list of NFP coordinators and family-life offices by state (see the Resources section that begins on page 45).

The price of classes varies from method to method. Many are covered by health insurance plans, especially if taught by a health care professional, so a couple may want to check with their insurance company before choosing a teacher.

NFP charting (gynecologic charting) is very useful for monitoring a woman's health. In choosing a teacher, women with irregular cycles, premenstrual syndrome, or other known gynecologic conditions may prefer a health care professional who knows what local health care is geared to use of the charting and supportive of NFP. Physicians, nurse practitioners, and physician's assistants can use the fertility charts as the basis of further investigation.

NFP and fertility-awareness methods (FAM) are not the same. Some FAMs are advertised as "natural contraception" or use fertility awareness to identify fertile times and then recommend using a barrier method (condom or diaphragm) during the fertile window. NFP's philosophical basis is quite different.

Choosing a Health Care Provider

Couples who use NFP appreciate having a health care provider who respects NFP and can read and interpret charting. Some areas have a number of physicians and nurses who are well educated in NFP (see page 46). Before an infertility work-up or pregnancy, a couple may want to discuss the teacher's knowledge and use of charting as well as basic attitudes regarding life and dignity of the person.

It's important they do this before they undergo tests. Some tests and procedures are not morally acceptable—medical technology should support the marriage, not the reverse. Plus, it's very difficult when a couple develops a relationship with a health care provider and then later discovers the professional doesn't support a Catholic approach to life issues.

Notes

1. United States Conference of Catholic Bishops. 2001. "Standards for Diocesan Natural Family Planning Ministry," p. 23. www.usccb.org/prolife/issues/nfp/Standards--USCCBBooklet.pdf (case sensitive; accessed April 3, 2009). Used with permission from the NFP Program, United States Conference of Catholic Bishops. All rights reserved.

2. World Health Organization. 1981. Task Force on Methods for the Determination of the Fertile Period, Special Programme of Research, Development and Research Training in Human Reproduction, "A Prospective Multicentre Trial of the Ovulation Method of Natural Family Planning, I, The Teaching Phase." *Fertility and Sterility,* 36:152–158.

3. Behre HM, Kuhlage J, Gassner C, et al. 2000. Prediction of ovulation by urinary hormone measurements with the home use ClearPlan® Fertility Monitor: Comparison with transvaginal ultrasound scans and serum hormone measurements. *Human Reproduction,* 15:2478–2482.

4. Kennedy KI and Trussell J. 2007. "Postpartum Contraception and Lactation." In: Hatcher RA, Trussell J, Nelson A, et al. *Contraceptive Technology,* Nineteenth Revised Edition. New York: Ardent Media, 403–409.

ARTIFICIAL CONTRACEPTION *and* STERILIZATION

As a nurse practitioner, I've encountered many Catholic couples who use or want to use contraceptives in spite of the Church's clear and consistent teaching that interfering with the natural outcome of marital relations is a grave sin. Once they make that choice, they're often focused only on the results—avoiding pregnancy—and are unaware of how contraceptives work. For example, they don't understand that instead of preventing pregnancy, some methods cause very early abortion.

As an NFP educator, I've encountered many couples already using contraceptives—Catholic and non-Catholic—who are surprised to learn what they weren't told and wish they'd asked more questions.

One couple, a Protestant minister and his wife, had used a variety of contraceptives: hormonal implants and injections, condoms, diaphragms, and oral contraceptives. They switched contraceptive methods because of an awareness of health effects, side effects, or inconvenience. As they prayed and informed themselves, they concluded that NFP was more fitting with their relationship with God and each other.

They had been married about twelve years when I came to know them and teach them NFP. On the third and final teaching session, the wife confided how much NFP had changed her marriage. She had come to know that physical affection from her husband during periods of abstinence was just that: affection. She didn't feel used as she had when she felt (feared) that every hug expressed his desire for intercourse. She no longer felt like an object.

Being informed about the effect of a substance on our bodies, our fertility, and our relationships makes such a difference on our decisions. This couple said they wished they'd known about NFP at the beginning of their marriage.

Artificial contraceptives come in two categories: *chemical* and *mechanical*. They rely on the physiologic aspect of the reproductive process by preventing the meeting of the sperm and egg. Most effort in this area has been directed toward interfering with the woman's reproductive processes, although pills that block sperm production are being tested.

As you read the following information, think not only about how the contraceptive works, but about the potential effects on the body and the relationship.

Chemical (Hormonal) Contraceptives

COMBINATION

The combination oral contraceptive pill (OCP) contains a synthetic *estrogen* (ethinyl estradiol or mestranol) and a synthetic *progestin* (norethindrone, norgestrel, or ethynodiol acetate) (Heffner, 2001).[1] Progestin, a synthetic hormone, is different from the naturally occurring hormone *progesterone*. In fact, where progesterone is a "pro-pregnancy" hormone that enriches the uterine lining, progestins cause the uterine lining to thin to the point that the fertilized ovum cannot implant. This is, in effect, an early abortion.

Combinations are also found in transdermal patches and vaginal rings. All combinations prevent pregnancy by

- suppressing ovulation (but not always—especially with low-dose formulations);
- slowing the egg's movement through the fallopian tube;
- thinning the uterine lining so the fertilized egg cannot implant (early abortion); and
- suppressing the cells of the cervix so the mucus is very thick and sperm cannot get through.

OCPs

OCPs were approved for use in the United States in 1959. The original formulations contained 200 mcg of synthetic estrogen. By the 1970s, dosages had dropped to 35 to 50 mcg of estrogen, and today's formulations typically contain 15 to 35 mcg. Many women died of heart attacks, blood clots, and strokes on the early formulations, but today's dosages are far safer. However, estrogen is a known cancer-causing agent.

Use of OCPs is undesirable or dangerous in women who smoke or who have a history of blood clots, deep venous thrombosis (DVT), stroke, heart attack, gallbladder disease, liver problems, diabetes, migraines, high blood pressure, and a family history of breast cancer, especially in a mother, sister, aunt, or grandmother. OCPs are associated with increased risk of premenopausal breast cancer, especially when used before a woman's first term pregnancy.[2]

Initially, OCPs were to be taken for three weeks and then followed by a week of sugar pills to imitate the woman's natural cycle and allow her to have a period. In 2005 this practice was challenged, and the extended-cycle OCP was approved by the United States Food and Drug Administration (FDA). The extended-cycle OCP can be taken continuously for three months followed by a week off to allow a withdrawal bleed.

OCPs that will eliminate menstrual periods altogether are being developed. The Society for Menstrual Cycle Research holds that this use of OCPs hasn't passed sufficient safety studies to justify their use as a lifestyle choice (as opposed to use for medical conditions) and criticizes what it perceives as negative portrayals of normal menstrual cycles in the manufacturers' promotional literature.[3]

Vaginal ring

Another format of combination estrogen and progestin is the vaginal ring, approved for use in 2001. The woman inserts the ring into her vagina, wears it for three weeks, and then discards it. After a week off to allow withdrawal bleeding, she inserts a new one. Side effects are similar to those of combination OCPs.

The ring is not suitable for women who have frequent vaginal irritations or infections. Use of the ring is also undesirable or dangerous in women who smoke or who have a history of blood clots, deep venous thrombosis (DVT), stroke, heart attack, gallbladder disease, liver problems, diabetes, migraines, high blood pressure, and a family history of breast cancer, especially in a mother, sister, aunt, or grandmother. [4, 5]

Transdermal patch

The transdermal patch is worn for three consecutive weeks and then removed for one week to allow withdrawal bleeding. In 2005 the FDA approved revised labeling to warn women that the product exposes women to higher levels of estrogen. In general, that may mean a higher level of the occurrence of blood clots. The patch is *not* as effective for women weighing more than 198 pounds.

PROGESTIN-ONLY

OCPs, injectable hormones, subdermal (beneath the skin) implants, and intrauterine devices, systems, or contraceptives (IUD, IUS, or IUC) are also available in *progestin-only* form.

OCPs

The progestin-only OCP, commonly referred to as the *minipill*, suppresses the luteinizing-hormone surge—and therefore ovulation—in some women. It also thickens the cervical mucus to block sperm from getting into the uterus, and it thins the lining of the uterus to prevent the fertilized egg from implanting. The postfertilization effects would have a greater concern for health professionals and women who consider this effect to be an early abortion.

Injectable hormones

Depo-Provera (medroxyprogesterone acetate; DMPA) is the brand name of a progestin approved by the FDA in 1992 as an injectable contraceptive. The injection is given every three months and within five days of the start of the menstrual period. The drug primarily inhibits ovulation but also thins the lining of the uterus.

DMPA can be used by women who cannot take estrogen or who require medication for seizures. The drug is fairly harsh, and while it doesn't permanently affect fertility, it can take a number of months for menstrual cycles to return to pre-DMPA patterns after a woman stops using it. Menstrual irregularities or no menstrual cycle are the main side effects. Other side effects include weight gain, mood swings, reduced sex drive, and headaches.

Implants

Currently only one type of implantable contraceptive system is available in the United States: *Implanon* (etonogestrel), a small, thin, implantable, single-rod hormonal contraceptive that is effective for up to three years. It was approved in 2006 by the FDA. The six-rod version with the brand name Norplant (levonorgestrel) was taken off the market in 2002.

Implanon can prevent pregnancy by suppressing ovulation in some women, but it also thickens the cervical mucus to block sperm from getting into the uterus, and it thins the lining of the uterus to prevent the fertilized egg from implanting (early abortion).

OTHER USES FOR OCPs AND AUTHENTIC WOMEN'S HEALTH CARE

OCPs are not inherently evil unless they're used as contraception, in which case the spouses are intentionally rejecting God's gift of fertility. Added to that is the chemical-abortion action of hormonal contraceptives and the subsequent loss of human life.

OCPs have been touted as having noncontraceptive benefits. Indeed, a variety of symptoms can be *managed* with OCPs, but OCPs do *not* cure disease or illness. The one true use for hormonal contraception is just that: contraception.

A number of gynecologic conditions that can be treated with an OCP can also be treated with cooperative hormonal therapy or other medications. While an OCP is recommended for management of some gynecologic conditions, the woman or couple should discuss alternatives with a gynecologic health care professional.

Think of the teenage girl with acne. An OCP is approved for use against acne, but it isn't offered to teenage boys—they're offered other forms of therapy. Women and parents of teenage girls may want to explore those options. In our sexually permissive society, some health care providers assume the OCP will treat the acne and prevent pregnancy without addressing the other social, psychological, and physical impacts of OCPs on a young woman.

Many women are advised that the OCP is the preferred treatment for irregular menstrual cycles, and they find themselves conflicted about using the OCP and doing what is morally acceptable. Instead of merely managing the cycles with OCPs, a provider of authentic women's health care diagnoses the reason for the irregular cycles.

OCPs are also associated with reductions in endometrial and ovarian cancer, but then so is pregnancy.

Side Effects

The side effects of OCPs can be numerous and varied. Entire books are dedicated to advising health care professionals on which OCP to switch their patients to if they're having side effects from another OCP.

Side effects may be due to estrogen, progestin, or both. Estrogenic effects include nausea, breast tenderness, and fluid retention. The most common side effect of progestin is bleeding irregularity.

Many women complain of mood changes and depression symptoms from either hormone. Some of this may be caused by OCP interference with the absorption of vitamin B_6 (pyridoxine).[6]

Sexual appetite is suppressed in some women who use OCPs. Researchers published an investigation measuring sex hormone–binding globulin (SHBG) before and after discontinuation of an OCP. Women with sexual dysfunction who had used OCPs had high levels of SHBG; even after OCP use was discontinued, SHBG did not decrease to the same levels as those of women who had never taken an OCP. The chronic elevation in SHBG levels may put women who use OCP at risk for long-term health problems, including sexual dysfunction.[7]

EMERGENCY CONTRACEPTION

Emergency contraceptive pills (ECPs), also called *morning-after pills,* prevent ovulation or fertilization and possibly work after fertilization to prevent implantation of a fertilized egg. Since ECPs act before implantation, they are medically and legally considered forms of contraception, but if the egg has been fertilized the ECP causes an early abortion. The scientific community has had considerable debate about this issue.

SPERMICIDES

A spermicide prevents pregnancy by killing sperm. Spermicides are available over the counter in the form of foams, creams, jellies, and suppositories that are placed in the vagina before intercourse. Nonoxynol-9, the major ingredient in most of these products, can irritate the vagina.

Mechanical Contraceptives

Most of these nonchemical devices prevent pregnancy by keeping sperm from fertilizing the egg. IUDs cause an early abortion by preventing fertilized eggs from implanting in the uterus.

CONDOMS

The *male condom* is a thin sheath of latex rubber, vinyl, or natural products which is placed on the erect penis.

The *female condom* is a thin, transparent, soft plastic lining that fits loosely inside a woman's vagina. It must be placed before intercourse and removed immediately after.

DIAPHRAGM

This soft latex cup covers the *cervix* (the part of the uterus that opens into the vagina). The rim of the diaphragm contains a firm, flexible spring that keeps it in place. Spermicide is placed inside the dome of the diaphragm before it's inserted into the vagina. The diaphragm prevents pregnancy by blocking sperm from entering the cervix; the spermicide kills or disables sperm. The diaphragm should be removed within twenty-four hours of intercourse.

Diaphragms must be fitted by a health care professional and rechecked for sizing with weight gain or loss of more than ten pounds and after childbirth or pelvic surgery. Women who use diaphragms have an increased rate of urinary tract infections and toxic shock syndrome.

CERVICAL CAP

This soft, deep, latex or plastic rubber cup is smaller than a diaphragm and snugly covers the *cervix* (the part of the uterus that opens into the vagina). Spermicide is put inside the cervical cap's dome before it's inserted into the vagina. The cervical cap prevents pregnancy by blocking sperm from entering the cervix; the spermicide kills or disables sperm. The cervical cap may be put in up to six hours before intercourse and left in for forty-eight hours.

Cervical caps must be fitted by a specifically trained provider and rechecked for sizing with weight gain or loss of more than ten pounds and after childbirth or pelvic surgery. Women who use cervical caps have an increased rate of urinary tract infections and toxic shock syndrome.

INTRAUTERINE DEVICES (IUD)

This mechanical contraceptive can also be hormonal. It's inserted into the uterus by a health care professional. It prevents pregnancy probably due to a combination of factors, one being that it irritates the lining of the uterus. This in turn decreases fallopian tube movement.

Two types are available: The *Paraguard Copper-T,* made of polyethylene with copper in the sleeves of each horizontal arm, can stay in place for ten years. The copper kills sperm. The *Mirena*'s polyethylene frame releases a daily 20-mcg dose of the synthetic hormone *progestogen* (levonorgestrel) for as long as five years.

In addition to the mechanical pregnancy-preventing action, IUDs containing progestin thicken cervical mucus and inhibit ovulation. When conception does occur, the IUD can cause an early abortion. The woman may not even be aware of it because it may not be distinguishable from a menstrual period.

Common side effects of IUD use include cramping and bleeding that diminish over time. IUD users are at an increased risk for pelvic infections, which in turn may lead to sterility.

It's interesting that in current advertising campaigns, IUDs (which are considered harmful in the American public's mind) are frequently called an intrauterine system (IUS) or intrauterine contraceptive (IUC).

Other Methods

Two other methods couples have used that are "unreliable" would include withdrawal (*coitus interruptus*) and douching after intercourse.

Any genital contact during the woman's fertile time may result in pregnancy. Even when the penis is withdrawn from the vagina just prior to ejaculation, seminal fluid can still be deposited and thereby lead to pregnancy. Once ejaculation occurs, it takes only minutes for the sperm to get into the cervix , cervical crypts, and uterus. Douching will not remove those sperm.

Sterilization

Some couples don't consider sterilization surgery to be a contraceptive, but it's actually the ultimate act of rejecting healthy fertility. Almost all sterilization techniques involve disrupting the normal anatomy that sperm and egg use to get to the uterus, permanently altering healthy reproductive organs to interfere with God's design for fertility.

Tubal ligation (having one's "tubes tied") is a permanent form of female sterilization in which the fallopian tubes are severed and sealed to prevent eggs from reaching the uterus. Hormone production, libido, and the menstrual cycle can be affected by tubal ligation. *Post-tubal ligation syndrome* (PTLS) results when blood volume to the ovaries decreases or is eliminated, causing a rapid decline of estrogen/progesterone levels. Many symptoms of PTLS are also associated with menopause, hormone shock, or estrogen/progesterone imbalance.

Essure is the brand name of a method in which tiny metal coils are placed in a woman's fallopian tubes. Over time, scar tissue that grows in and around these coils blocks the tubes so sperm can't reach the eggs. Unlike tubal ligation, Essure doesn't require surgery, the tubes are not cut, and it cannot be reversed. If pregnancy occurs after the coils are implanted, it will most likely take place in a fallopian tube (ectopic pregnancy).

Vasectomy is a surgical procedure in which the *vas deferens* are cut to obstruct the passage of sperm. The sperm produced before the procedure are still alive and available, so the man is still fertile until they're gone. This takes about three months for most men. The operative procedure itself is safely performed in an out-patient surgery center and doesn't require general anesthesia. However, significant long-term changes can occur, such as autoimmune reactions to sperm. After vasectomy, the blood-testis barrier is broken, and 60 percent to 70 percent of men form antibodies to sperm. This autoimmune reaction sometimes triggers pain that can be limited to the testicular area or may be more widespread. *Postvasectomy pain syndrome*, a chronic and sometimes debilitating condition, may develop up to several years after vasectomy.[8-10]

Regret is a common side-effect of all methods of sterilization. High-cost microsurgery techniques are used to reverse surgical sterilization in men and women. The functional success rates vary widely—generally, surgical sterilization is permanent. The Essure procedure cannot be reversed.

Effectiveness of Family-Planning Methods

All of the methods presented here have established effectiveness rates, but those can be misleading because they're based on perfect or theoretical use. Effectiveness rates are approached two ways:

- *Perfect-use* or *correct-use rate:* the number of unintended pregnancies that occur when the method is used consistently and according to instructions.
- *Typical-use rate:* the combined number of unintended pregnancies that occur when the method is followed correctly *and* when users don't always follow the method correctly.

Several problems are inherent in studies of effectiveness. The first is that a couple's intentions may not be either to avoid or to achieve a pregnancy. Some feel strongly one way or the other; some are open to pregnancy but may not be quite ready to say "we're trying to have a baby," so they knowingly use the fertile time or may be careless in following the method.

No method, natural or artificial, is 100 percent effective in avoiding pregnancy. The effectiveness of NFP is affected by the experience of the couple as well as the expertise of the NFP teacher. When couples understand the methods and are motivated to follow them, NFP is 95 percent to 99 percent successful in spacing or limiting births.

For couples who don't follow all the rules for avoiding pregnancy, two to fifteen will be pregnant in a year. This number may be higher for couples who have difficulty reading their fertility signs because of breastfeeding or perimenopause.[11]

Notes

1. Dickey, Richard P. 2007. *Managing Contraceptive Pill Patients*, Thirteenth Edition. Dallas: EMIS, page 130.
2. Kahlenborn C, Modugno F, Potter DM, Severs WB. 2006. Oral Contraceptive Use As a Risk Factor for Premenopausal Breast Cancer: A Meta-Analysis. *Mayo Clinic Proceedings* (October), 81:1290–1302.
3. Society for Menstrual Cycle Research. 2007. Position Statement: "Menstruation Is Not A Disease." http://menstruationresearch.org/position/menstrual-suppression-new-2007/ (accessed April 3, 2009).
4. Kahlenborn, et al.
5. Johansson EDB and Sitruk-Ware R. 2004. New delivery systems in contraception: Vaginal rings. *American Journal of Obstetrics and Gynecology*, 190:S54–S59.
6. Dickey.
7. Panzer CW, Sarah F, Gemma K, et al. 2006. Impact of oral contraceptives on sex hormone–binding globulin and androgen levels: a retrospective study in women with sexual dysfunction. *Journal of Sexual Medicine*, 3(1):104–113.
8. Nangia AK, Myles JL, Thomas AJ Jr. 2000. Vasectomy reversal

for the post-vasectomy pain syndrome: a clinical and histological evaluation. *The Journal of Urology*, 164:1939-1942.

9. McMahon AJ, Buckley J, Taylor A, et al. 1992. Chronic testicular pain following vasectomy. *British Journal of Urology*, 69(2):188–191.

10. Choe J and Kirkemo A. 1996. Questionnaire-based outcomes study of nononcological post-vasectomy complications. *The Journal of Urology*, 155(4):1284-1286.

11. Fehring R, Kitchen S, Shivanandan M. 1999. "An Introduction to Natural Family Planning." Washington, DC: Diocesan Development Program for Natural Family Planning, United States Conference of Catholic Bishops. www.usccb.org/prolife/issues/nfp/intronfp.shtml#5 (accessed April 3, 2009).

RESOURCES

Diocesan Resources

Information about NFP classes in your area is available from your diocesan office of Marriage and Family Life. In some dioceses, NFP programs can be found in a Catholic hospital, the offices of Respect life activities, pastoral programs, or Catholic Charities. If you're not sure whom to call in your diocese, contact

Natural Family Planning Program
Secretariat for Laity, Marriage, Family Life & Youth
3211 4th Street NE
Washington, DC 20017
202-541-3040
www.usccb.org/prolife/issues/nfp/

General Information

One More Soul
1846 N. Main St.
Dayton OH 45405
800-307-7685
www.omsoul.com/nfp-only.php

Hormonal-Monitoring Method (Marquette Method)

Marquette University
College of Nursing
Institute for NFP
P.O. Box 1881
Milwaukee, WI 53201-1881
414-288-3854
http://nfp.marquette.edu/

Saint Louis University
Nursing Center for Fertility Education
3525 Caroline St.
St. Louis, MO 64104-1099
877-977-8950
www.slu.edu/x19845.xml

Ovulation Method

Billings Ovulation Method Association
PO Box 2135
St. Cloud, MN 56302
651-699-8139
www.boma-usa.org

Family of the Americas Foundation
PO Box 1170
Dunkirk, MD 20754
301-627-3346
www.familyplanning.net

Pope Paul VI Institute for the Study of Human Reproduction
(Creighton Model Fertility*Care*)
6901 Mercy Road
Omaha, NE 68106
402-390-6600
www.popepaulvi.com

Sympto-thermal Method

Couple to Couple League
PO Box 111184
Cincinnati, OH 45211-1184
513-471-2000
www.ccli.org

Northwest Family Services, Inc.
4805 NE Glisan Street
Portland, OR 97213
503-215-6377
www.nwfs.org